THE TUMBLING SKY

The Tumbling Sky

Doris Corti

HEADLAND

First published in 1998
by
HEADLAND PUBLICATIONS
38 York Avenue, West Kirby,
Wirral, Merseyside. L48 3JF

A full CIP record for this book is available
from the British Library

ISBN 1 902096 32 0

HEADLAND acknowledges the financial
assistance of North West Arts Board

Printed in Great Britain by
L. Cocker & Co., Berry Street, Liverpool

CONTENTS

for my family

'Nothing is worth more than this day.'
— **Goethe**

THE TUMBLING SKY

The unicorn
prances in a tree-fringed field.

To suddenly see the white body,
to want to get near, to want
with the same urgency as a need to breathe,

a delicious madness to chase a myth,

there is no mistaking the spiralled horn.
I have to follow
as it moves into the folded hills
where the sky tumbles down to meet the ground.

Its mane, a white silk pennant,
diminishes from sight,
everything else is reduced in this transient moment

and the unicorn, lost like the holy grail,
vanishes into the remoteness of doubt.

AUTUMN

Leaves hide, curl and die in mounds
across lawns and pavements,
    in suburbs
        and cities,
on open farmland, and the concrete areas
of high-rise flats.

Leaves drift along walkways of past lives,
    merge into the daily detritus,
        their movements gentle
            as sighs.

Softly they crowd into corners and areas,
    curl under our feet
sometimes unnoticed, they sink into earth
    little by little,
        lighter than breezes
mildewed and powdery, vanish in crevices,
carrying somewhere their flutters and echoes.

QUICKSILVER

The moon has dipped into the sea tonight
quicksilvering it,

mirrored, it caresses the seal smooth sleekness,

light penetrates,
and sleeping mermaids flick their sequined tails
scattering spangled dreams across the shore,

while the moon devours the sea.

SMALL EVENTS

Thin, scratched lines
on the face of a dead moon,
screech of owl invades moorland silence
winged urgency vibrates like a small night wind.

The ewe, throb of insistence in her belly
shelters behind granite,
ice-capped lair of sabre-toothed,
sullen land-mark, ironbound to earth.

A cloud drifts across the moon,

the ewe shudders, a heaving dark mound.
Blood smears pattern earth, trace a shadow
beneath the pulsing wet of newborn lamb.

Dawn, not sudden, diffuses light
into a grey landscape,
spreads a recurring hope.

The lamb stumbles,
repeats the plea in its throat
juddering cold air,
and seeks familiar scents to suck vitality.

IN THE BEGINNING

We could tread delicately,

moving with light steps
between the trees,

respecting the silence
and soft light their
interwoven branches cloister.

We could acknowledge
their superior age by laying
our fingertips upon the grained bark,
and smoothing

with an almost gentle reverence.

We should lower our voices
awed by their immensity,
drifting our senses into another time

to primaeval beginnings,
to root and seed,

establish a oneness
with their majesty,
and span the star time
of eternity

breathing their own elixir.

TODAY

autumn burns into fenland fields that stretch
rippled, like dark seas, to the skyline.

End of year colours alternate under shifting clouds,
a tractor, leggo like, trundles into the distance.

Moving along a straight road on the bus
we seem to be edging towards space,
but never nearer the horizon.

On the seat beside me, the old man, tucked and weathered
as the fields he'd tilled, appears to be waiting,
is alert to some secret signal as we pass
the long line of poplars edging the road.

And suddenly they are upon us,
somewhere between Guymans and Fen End the wild geese
soar,
arcing into a pattern of delight as we watch
through the windscreen.

Two dozen, wings outstretched, and six more,
the guardians, two foot behind.
Felt tip marks on a colour washed sky,
their beauty acknowledged by our excited murmurings.

Undeniably they have established a right
to this flight path.

The old man leans forward watching their exodus.

ALL IN A DAY

'It could have been....'
the thought made mockery of logic day
begun so evenly with normal preparations,

the inter-city train to work,
a carriage with its usual unseen faces
behind the morning headlines.

I side-stepped legs, briefcase or two,
saw a slight smile on someone's face
and answered with my own.

Less than an hour, King's Cross
and no turning back, his card within my hand,
telephone number - lunch - decisions undertaken.

Outside the station, too many roads diverge,
so many people cross my path,

past years the same,
but now the present gets in the way,
allows no time for this ...

next day avoiding the usual 9.15, I take a later train,
still hanker after what might have been.

WORDS

Elusive as wisps of smoke,
Words will not thread today.
They tangle without hope

Of ever finding a reasoned way,
And choke on clichéd crumbs
of conversations, keep dreams at bay.

Lingering in cafés in a hub of tongues
We join in chatter without aim,
You and I are now the lonely ones

Who speak nothings, making nothing plain
Carefully avoid phrases that are wise,
And are lured into a dishonest game.

Your words and mine will never synchronize,
We babble, avoiding speech and our goodbyes.

LIKE LAZARUS

I am woman, risen like Lazarus
from some nether-world,
a small, or deep sleep will do it,

risen now, to understand,
and to know that reality
is mother-of-pearl fragile,
can crumble silently, like sand,
changing known shapes.

I collect fragments
sift through particles,
searching for the sheen of pearl,
that like truth, is sometimes hidden.

A CLOSER LOOK

Look closely, a snail is not impenetrable,
hold one up to the light,
see, it is fragile,

little grooves, some thinner than others
make it vulnerable. Unable to escape your prying
it will keep still,
a whirled shell on the palm of your hand.

Enclosed, the soft body appears secure,
hidden, it is still the prey of predators
and Iago-like whispers that incite to squeeze.

Snails are not sacrosanct, their shells are crushable.

DISCOVERY

This morning is a sonnet,
summer high
with threads of dreams trailing
through all our conversation over breakfast,

which we take on the patio
beside the trellised honeysuckle
and green, with the sun bordering silver birch
and pine trees;

hot croissants
and coffee,
and the sun, passion hot already
loops into the progression of a poem,
as words and laughter blend
easy as the butter tasting creamy.

We explore our way
through sentences and phrases, stumbling
but no longer tentative,
carefully assembling what we have come to know.

Our words dance in sunlight,
and revive silences, as full awareness
is structured in a theme.

THE CAULDRON

I have seen leaden waves punishing the quay,
and rising through a dragon's breath of mist,
heard groaning pebbles gleaned into an awesome tryst;
a sea hell-raked with cold, metallic grey
advancing like some predator at the start of day.
Yet, from this same shore I have seen amethyst
splinter cloud, and heard the subtle thrust
of fragmenting waves wash the shingled bay.

I have touched its damask green,
and shot silk blue, mysterious and sleek.
Caught fantasies of coral depths, a silver line,
winding strands, and pearl shine gleam;
watched the sea gather sun into a cauldron deep,
and felt each moon tugging into time.

AN OBSERVATION

Today the world stood still,
its axis ceased turning, and here we hang
like flies in a spun web.

The moon and the sun are at strange angles
a few stars still shine.

I can't come to terms with this situation,
the flood was different, Noah had known all along
and built his ark.

I watch the hat-stand in the hall topple
and umbrellas and hats suddenly
sprout from odd corners.

The moon and the sun are at strange angles
a few stars still shine.

I'm afraid that the moon and the sun and I,
will drown together in a strange blue pool
but the worn, brown edge of the ark might slide
into view, and perhaps the lark from my garden
will fly past me singing.

The moon and the sun are at strange angles
a few stars still shine.

STONE CIRCLE

A circle of white stones and a bleached sky,
In winds that hone the mind and herald snow,
A constant question, and a lone bird's cry —
                                                    an ache to know.

A litany, repetitive, clear, and slow
Threads through the stones as stars turn in the sky,
Shadows of old truths glimpsed as moons hang low.

An incantation in the cold wind's sigh
Of whispered echoes here from long ago,
Drawn through time's space, this haunting constant cry —
                                                    an ache to know.

MORNING

Light, thin as November air, creeps a narrow line
around the window frame.
Outside, the spindle tops of conifers congregate
like wizards.

At night, outlines of pine chest, pictures,
lamp and clock, become comforters,
now, the widening line of light intrudes,
and half seen things become real. Lying stiffly
we wait for the punishing sound of the alarm,
and watch dark trees bruise the window pane.

Today, like yesterday, begins with small sounds.
We wait for the heavy thud of newspaper upon the mat,
the postbox with its clamour, until the milkman's van,
a noisy hearse, comes trundling....

THE WAITING

A tracery of mist outlines the park
where snowdrops swarm, and over by the swings
small children soar to vapoured heights
touching their own heavens, and make loud
utterances of joy,

while I, on a park bench, huddled against the damp
of winter rawness, am waiting for the Spring and
Summer of a poem. An hour ago, when the waiting
was a new beginning, and green,
small heads of bulbs brought some assurance,
I swung on my arc of thought
like a child rejoicing.

It will not come. Thin light widens between railings
and trees, laurel bushes smudge the day, crows mock,
and snowdrops flaunt their early show;
but none of this reality persuades a poem to live,

the warp and weft of images dissolve, sieved
through shrubs and grass like mist
leaving a vision's wraith.

A LATE SPRING

The rooks are silent on peaks of trees,
and although the calendar states spring and summer time
the sky disputes,
clouds of unshed tears keep day-time dim,

the radio turned low
brings weather forecasts
a quiet voice speaks of gloom to come;

yet, through the wide window framing my kitchen
and my thoughts,
I see the living earth
the verdant green,
as rain spatters violently on glass,

trees move in the wind,
their tops touching clouds that shift
and lighten as I watch.

FRAGILITY

The air screams a sharp new breath,
is alive,

lawns, quagmired, untrimmed with choking weeds,
are not the dainty touches suburbia has come to know;

brow-beaten, their petals scattered
red as death-drops, tulips are diminished,
this is not the expected Springtime;

even now,
even as sunlight shoves its way through a determined cloud force
their proudness reduced, little swans dying,
pigments of colour bleeding into wet earth.

TANGO TIME

A tipsy wind sang in the trees last night,
snapped sinewed boughs,
a discordant symphony that pricked at nerves
and scraped through my brain
disrupting sleep,

the distant sea caught the same wild song,
leapt, writhed, crashed cymbals sounds
against the rocks, took my mind a dance,

and the white, scythed moon
cut clean into my room
mirrored on glass,
halved my head, so that one part sang
and one part wept,

and the part that wept,
dreamed a lily wreath round my head,
and the other part sang
and danced all night in frantic tango-time,
danced away with the wind,
and never returned.

SHADOWS

All day rain barbs strike on windows
the car windscreen is a flood;

the silent birds leave scattered crumbs
on feeding tables,
and the ghosts of old roses
fall battered from their stems.

Inside warm rooms we hear the rain
scratching on outside walls, tippling down gutters.
This scratching has become quieter, and now
is cat's purr soft.

An early twilight, the television screen flickers
in a darkening room,
someone is talking, mouthing humour,
no replies needed.

Buttoned to the chin, like a child by its mother,
I leave the cosy hug of home
to loiter on rain-washed paving slabs, and walk
reminding myself of freshly wet pebbled beaches,
and the surge of sea.

A keen, small wind, shakes off the threat of day.
I move from lamplight to lamplight, and my shadow
like a small form of thought, follows me,
moves as I move, waits for me, turns as I turn,
a flattening out of what I thought I knew.

LE CRI
(Bronze Head by Auguste Rodin 1898) Paris, Musee.

Distanced from fear, we stare
at the woman.

Channelled through moulded lines in bronze
her hollow eyes stare back, sinewed neck
and throat show a stifled scream.

In the corners of that quiet room,
coming upon her silent grief
we feel intruders. Did love drive her mad,
yet fill her days with promises?

What fears revolved round all her minutes?
Some power, unspoken, possessed her thoughts,
tainted her love, sealed her lips, and gave back
only emptiness.

The lines on bronze diminish nothing,
show us her soul confined within a scream,
and the cruel intensity of madness.

VOICES

In the darkness of the shed I cannot hear the calls
of others who are playing in the game;
through a mere slit, a sliver of light falls.

Outside, soft sound of rain, murmurings and footfalls,
inside, smells of damp earth, and nothing seems the same.
In the darkness of the shed I cannot hear the calls.

The wooden shelves hold twine bundles, and string balls
there is nothing more, no labels here, and no names;
through a mere slit, a sliver of light falls.

I need the knife-like blade of light, this blackness palls
the scent of dank earth relates the inadequacy of fame.
In the darkness of the shed I cannot hear the calls.

I recall old myths, and legends told in halls
by ancient Celts, by Saxons, and by Danes.
Through a mere slit, a sliver of light falls.

Confined inside this dimness and the wooden walls,
the reassurance of voices needs to be made plain;
in the darkness of the shed I cannot hear the calls;
through a mere slit, a sliver of light falls.

THE MANAGER'S ANNUAL REPORT
(For P.N.)

'A poem is a dream.' He said.
'It is not tangible, not real.'

Staring across the desk at him,
seeing his face, small,
as through the spy-hole in his door
I thought, 'He's telling me it's a waste of time
to write a poem, to let a dream surface.'

The other things he said reminded me
that with him I earned my daily bread.
I felt the solid walls close in on me
like coffin lids.

He wanted to shatter my dreams.
How could he know that in them I touch the stars,
and garland the moon with flowers?

Watching him later, smiling his way between desks,
my hatred turned to sadness, for what he missed.

FINGERS CROSSED

Little wind, but sunlight spangles frosted pavements.
Bright-eyed the next door woman
attacks small pieces of litter, mostly sweet wrappers
dropped by passing children. We smile, nod,
and acknowledge sunshine.

Wrapped in warmth, layers of wool,
cardigan and coat, I am immune from cold
and desperation, or the quiet part of it that fills
so many lives. I tell myself this, mouthing hope
into a stranglehold of scarf; remember the look
in the eyes of a stranger waiting to confide,

and on the train, (the two hour run to Lincolnshire),
the woman with the worried look, who sipped her coffee
in the plastic cup and asked the time continually.

Later on, marshmallow clouds are gradually absorbed
into a murky afternoon, and accompanying children
on the home run from school, I hear the eagerness
of shouts, watch the sorting out of sweets,
join in their laughter, and carefully side-step
to avoid cracks between paving stones.

BAG LADY

She paused inside the café door,
tugging at her tattered coat.
Then grinning, shambled her way to me,
exuding gin, and body heat.

I saw the washed out blue of eyes
across the table-top, skin grimed with city filth.
She spoke of places she found warm
to sleep in, words drivelling from her mouth.

'They turn you out from libraries.'
She said, shrugging officialdom away.
Then, moving her yellowing face closer, confided,
'I read of God in there today.'

In the room, a sudden pause in conversations,
a curtained embarrassment, eyes avoiding my face;
until a small normality returned — in sounds,
cups placed in saucers, clatter of knives on plates.

Hurriedly I gathered handbag, umbrella, gloves,
trappings of an existence outside hers.
Watching she asked suddenly, 'Who is the Messiah?'
High-pitched her voice vibrated round the walls.

The room, animated, made way for me.
I fled round awkward corners, no answer on my tongue.
Heard her calling after my retreating back,
'When will he come?'

MY FATHER

He watched the curves and straights
of all my writing,
hoping one day for magnificence,
like seeing water changed into wine.

His angularity in the small room
was strangely comforting.
He left me space to search through silences
allowing words to come uncrowded on the page,

and time was an unhurried walk into a garden.

Then later, he jogged my memory
with song, lines from poems and the psalms;

he waited, accepting the stridence of my adolescence.

Little by little, applying my pen,
I scrabbled through syllables, rhythms and words,
never quite managing a miracle.

Even without his presence in my room,
I have the (secret) sense that writing symbols,
plucking at lines and phrases, turning them around,
might somehow achieve something remarkable.

THE CRAFTSMAN
(Pompeii)

The bowl's preciseness fits neatly between cupped hands,
instinctively our fingers want to mould the shape,
and feel a thumb's impression on the curve.

Did the potter dream as he worked,
listened to dogs barking,
and children playing beside his open door?

Did he dream of life beyond the Roman road,
his fingers curving a well for holding clustered grapes,
ripe figs, pomegranates,
and apples from the sacred tree?

Did he dream that in a thousand years,
other hands would want to span this curve,
and close as snugly as his own around a parable of time?

THE CELT

As he spoke it was music,
sang its way into my heart, the lilt
and the stresses fine ripples of a tune
that sprang before language,

a time of trees, and water, and wind.

A fire in this music,
a passion of old songs that held cadences
and inflections, like landscapes of magnificence,

and as he spoke,
merely a recognition and a greeting, the seas
and tides, and old myths surfaced,
broke on the crest of a thought
that held whispers of the ancients.

WAITING TO BE MET
(An Evacuee - 1940)

A child, too big to cry
I'd grown up in that year of war,
'was old enough' they said
to travel far; loneliness, a familiar friend,
came with me. The guard had helped me
to descend, unloading bag and me, clutching
my gas-mask in its cardboard box, the pocket game.
He'd asked, in his country drawl,
'You know her name?'
He meant the woman coming to collect me.
No-one came.

The silence was immense
after the train had gone;
late sunlight daubed the wooden seat,
the picket fence, against which I leant
too big to cry, and waited.
No-one came.

I thought I heard a clock chime five
tolling into emptiness and fear;
then footsteps hurrying near, and through the gate
the woman came, unsmiling,
to take me to her home.
I stayed two years, but even now,
it seems upon reflection, that
no-one ever came at Trowbridge Station.

TRAVELLERS

Where shall we go my love, my love?
Shall we go where the air is cool,
or stand on a shore of coral sand,
while the sun drips blood on the sea?

Will we see the nightingale on the thorn,
or shall we hear only the song
while the moon burns a hole
in the deep stretch of night,
and I curl like a cat in your arms?

Maybe we will walk in cloistered paths
through a flame of fallen leaves,
and I shall hide the myrrh in a jar on the shelf,
give you a leaf from a myrtle tree
to set the seal of my heart on our life.

OLD LADY SINGING

Such a time of it she had that day, singing
in the quiet afternoon to other residents
who sat like threaded beads around the room.

A little song of all her joy
she offered them. Some smiled, others still as death
waited, and then, some nodded in time to the loud,
unstructured rhythm of her tune.

Such a time of it she had, weaving her song,
linking past and present into a ballad
of cascading happiness.
Such joy she shared that afternoon.

HYACINTHS

Blue and white, in a green-glazed bowl
they bloomed
on her window sill;

each gaping, waxen, floret mouth
exuded a funereal perfume.

After I had closed her eyelids,
attended to all the tasks that follow on a death,
I felt their sap strong in stems,
and hated them still living.

'A candelabrum' someone said, admiringly.
For me, they held the sour scent of death - was glad
when rust edged each star shaped mouth.

Their incense lingered in my mother's room,
more pungent than the bitterness of myrrh.

THE REUNION

Thoughts cut scalpelwise, slicing deep
into complacent conversation;
four of us in the restaurant corner,
dark with no window, we observe each other,
our voices tick into time.

Sitting here, I watch you turn – your face half hidden
in the shadow; you are aware that I am watching,
and to please me, smile; the pain shows
in lines around your eyes, I say nothing,
their muted voices are a cliché.

How can they know, the others,
what has been said or savoured?
They merely acknowledge his absence,
pulling their chairs closer.

The wine before food restores us;
we talk more loudly, a shrugging of shoulders
as we linger on wine-sips of memory we cannot avoid;

and presently, we eat and laugh a little,
the wine in the decanter - house wine, dry as crucifixion
vinegar zaps into our veins, and we say his name
like calling the roll.

FAMILIAR PATTERNS

Glancing backwards into time, I savour images,
the kitchen, and wide window, with light reflecting
on painted walls. My mother's smile, like a candleflame welcome,
the bowl in her hand, and the rhythmic mixing,

everything centred on that preciseness, as if the world
were caught in a soft moment, where I fit easily
into the weave of familiar patterns,
touch blue-bordered china, close my hands round thin cups,
crumble freshly baked bread, fill a stone bowl with water,
a jug with sweet peas.

I drift my thoughts, counting them, like beads in a rosary.

SUNFLOWERS
(Vincent van Gogh)

They flaunt themselves, voluptuously,
a strident reality. They burn the eyes,
a frenzied truth, glowing in gold certainty,

life masquerading in flowers, revered seed heads,
coronets of aztec priests,

they are the sunlight he captured, filling his space
of time, and his intensity still burns
like some long remembered vow.

FLOWERS
(A painting by David Bomberg)

From across the room, and the gap
dividing us, your world cajoles me.

My senses are projected into a whirling mass
of colour, that transforms
flower heads to a single vibrancy.

There is promise in such ecstasy,
a sensual delight that dominates the frame,

and yet, I stay upon the threshold
of my uncertainty.

I would enter your land, but need time,

I am unwilling to be persuaded
into the dimension you are showing,

I would need to forsake the familiar paths
of my own realities,
to grasp the dominance of your thought.

STOKE FLEMING
(South Devon)

Old, we should continue searching,
in legends,
caves of dragons,

in the wave, scented thyme,
wild primroses, and rain.

Sometimes, trawl in our line to stars,
and wait listening,
through the void, the dark mind, through deep waters
and shadows, hills of eagles, forests,
and mountain silences;

wait, for the bright spectrum,
the curve of dreams.

LEAVE-TAKING

The lane where the honeysuckle grows
ends in blue,

blue skies and delphiniums, the painted door,
blue plates and damsons,
juice staining the fine surface as ripeness
burst through their skins,
unripened globules when I 'd left.

'Not long', you'd said. 'Only a week or so?'
Your eyes inferred a hidden fear.

You never said, 'don't leave',
merely closed the newly painted door.

It took a while to walk the lane,
a pause halfway - a turning back,

but that day the blueness was not distinct,
only a fuzzy colour wash, insipid,
and not quite real, like all of what we had,
what we had known.

PRAWLE POINT

Water, like pewter, silver dull
reflects a dour month - March, and rain slants
needle-wise into our faces so that we gasp
toiling up Prawle Point, through lanes wreathed
with blackthorn's Easter blossoming.

Sheep stare at our approach then move
to higher paths, primroses still bloom, and I recall
last year you said,
     'they look like clumps of scattered sun.'

It was easier then, matching my step to your stride.
I miss you,
miss sheltering under sea-smooth rocks
miss your body shielding mine against the gale's thrust.

The others understand my sudden silences,
call across areas of raw red earth
the wind bringing only their endings
     'not far,
      keep going...'

At the highest point waves back up
against tooth-edged rocks, the cliffs vibrate with them,
and sea-spray like tears, tastes salt in my memory.

THE PICNIC

was a disaster
    a mistake
to eat by the lake where mosquitoes dived,

their incessant thrum
under the searing sun detracting from romance,
the sting in your final words biting more closely
than their needle barbs;

the venom in their attack
nothing to the sting
    of what you said,
the angry turn of your head, the walking away
out of the day, and my life,

    the mosquitoes homing in
on the cream and sweetness.

THE PENTACLE

Ripples in pools shatter my image
the willow hangs frozen.

Here, in this room, a silent recovery
pictures hang firmly, square against white walls.

Here I am safe from the breaking of idols;
I listen to your quiet breathing, and the page that you turn.

Outside, the air is alive with the keening of old griefs,
wind through the apple tree threatens the boughs.

Inside the pentacle I sit stitching a fine seam
softness of silk under my hands; sewing and stitching
I weave my own safety, thread the silver of sadness
into a needle - sure of myself, of the next stitch, of cutting.

Here in the room, lamps glow reassuringly,
while from a curl in the shadows the serpent unfurls.

THE LOST TIDES
(Fenlands)

Earth quickens under dyke roads,
draws sustenance from the salt of secrets.

Each moon keeps the secret, tugs at tides
and the channelled run by hidden shores,
forgotten sea, and marshland dune.

White, belligerent clouds dominate black fields
and space; against the skyline, like projected film,
a boy and his dog leap on a dyke road
playing age-old rituals of run, and chase.

A curious beauty here, in light undiminished
by shadows of trees and hills. Only the gulls
know the secret ways, where air
stings salt over ploughed drills.
They follow lost tides, skimming the air
with wings unfurled, sky-gliding,

while the boy embraces the day
and the turning moon still rides.

NORTH BY NORTH-EAST

The wind
honed our fury
to spike-edged words,

trailing
on a breath of ice,
like frightened birds.

Shrouded,
the winter sun
eclipsed from us.

We screamed
our isolation
into that open place,

echoes
passed into
the silences of time,

the wind
snatching the remnants
of our dying.

THE PEACOCK EPISODE

From the dark mouth of the tunnel
a peacock stepped, stood on the railway track
surveying us, tail drooping on dusty ground.

We stared at him from platform five,
our gasps rippling along the line. He turned
flaunting green and blueness, displaying feathered,
mohican crest, and like some flamboyant tribesman
held our gaze unblinkingly.

Only the slightest movement of his claws
hinted at the direction of his path, and brought him
nearer to where we stood.

A red-faced man, (railway officialdom),
hurried down the steps. 'We've alerted all the trains',
he reassured the line of us,
drawn up like silent soldiers.

A colourful poem that peacock, invading
the dusty atmosphere,

and all along the line we held our breath.
Two men emerged from the tunnel's depths,
and netted the bird, whose raucous cries
enlivened Monday morning's drabness..

BARBADOS

The sugar cane seems to grow
a yard or so after the rain, and purple, pink,
and bronze bougainvillaea marble outside walls.
Palm trees, feathered and fishtail,
span spaces between skyline and white fences.

The area of sky is higher, wider, and shifting patterns
of light mosaic the lawn,
hibiscus glow, and the peewit's call is as triumphant
as the distant cockerel's crow.

A dog barks far away, emphasising the stillness.
Casuarina trees bend uniformly, shaped as if in prayer,
and incense from frangipani petals drifts across to me.

I recline as still as the small lizard nearby,
warm, silk air strokes my skin,
a late benediction, as the earth rotates.

BARBADOS
(Night-time)

How strange, tonight there are no stars,
headlights on distant cars flash like fireflies,
but the sky is dark, draped velvet.

An aeroplane meanders across, from west to east
its tail-lights tattooing green and red,
an artificial tinselling of night;

no star, or moon predominates, and the density of purple
outwits the clustered lights on distant houses.

Darkness brings a night-sky loneliness.

SLAPTON SANDS

Back to the beginning, or so it seems
on Slapton Sands in the evening,
before night drops like a damp cloak
over distant hills, and shingled paths.

Walking along the beach, the hypnotic rhythms
of waves become part of myself, the indentations
of raindrops on water create small patterns,
and are gathered into the continuing rhythm;

the light diminishes, and trees on the headland
are not trees, but black smudges. This morning, there
was an exultation of light, splinters of sun on water,
and long sandbar shadows.

There is still enough light to see fronds of seaweed
patterning the shoreline, the small, empty crab shells
and stones of varying sizes, that bleached and honed
have a beauty like the stars,

a continuing beauty, like the book of hours.

ACKNOWLEDGEMENTS

Some of these poems have appeared in *Acumen, Envoi, Writing Poetry, Windfall, The Moon is a letter 'C', Marigolds Grow Wild on Platforms, Rituals & Reminders, The Space Between.*

'Hyacinths' won the Society of Women Writers & Journalists Centenary Poetry Competition (1994).